Plant and Animal Partners

BY NATALIE LUNIS

Table of Contents

How Are Plants and Animals Connected?

The world of nature is like a web. Every part is connected in some way to every other part. Every living thing depends on other living things to survive.

Plants and animals are connected to each other in their need for food. This link is known as a **food chain**.

An Arctic Tundra Food Chain

Sun   Plant   Arctic hare   Arctic fox

▲ A green plant uses sunlight to make food. The plant is eaten by the Arctic hare which, in turn gets eaten by the Arctic fox.

Some plants and animals are connected in other ways, too. They act as partners and help each other survive.

▲ Sloths and tiny green plants called algae help each other. Algae grow on the sloth's hair. This helps the sloth blend in among the green trees.

HOW Do Plants and Birds Help Each Other?

Birds help plants by spreading the plants' **pollen**. Many plants have brightly colored petals, sweet-smelling **nectar**, or perfumed scents that attract birds.

BEAT That!

Hummingbirds beat their wings so fast that they can drink nectar without even landing on the flower.

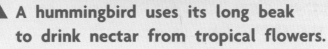

▲ A hummingbird uses its long beak to drink nectar from tropical flowers.

Birds sometimes form one-sided partnerships with other animals. A cattle egret hangs around rhinos and other large animals. As it walks, the rhino disturbs insects that live in the ground. The egret eats the insects.

◀ **A parrot eats this plant's fruit, then scatters the seeds in its droppings.**

Some plants have sweet fruits that attract birds. Inside the fruits are seeds. After the birds enjoy a tasty meal, they scatter the fruits' seeds in their droppings. These seeds then grow into new plants.

HOW Do Plants and Insects Help Each Other?

Bees help flowering plants, too. Each time a bee visits a flower to gather nectar, the plant's pollen sticks to the bee's body.

bee's tongue used for sipping nectar

pollen grains on bee

pollen grains on flower

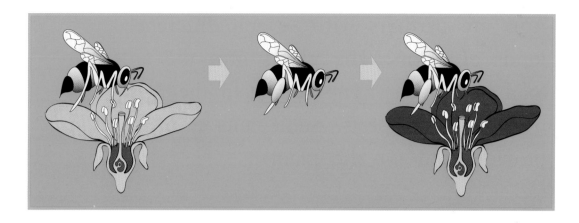

When the bee moves on to another flower, some of the pollen from the first plant rubs off on the next plant.

Each flower that the bee visits needs pollen from another flower in order to make seeds. So, as the bee gathers food for itself, it also helps the flower produce seeds that will grow into new plants.

Can you think of another insect that helps to spread pollen?

Ants are partners with several different kinds of plants. The plants give the ants food and shelter. The ants help the plants by scaring off pests. Some ants even provide food for the plant.

▲ In South America, Azteca ants and cecropia trees live together. The trees' leaves provide food for the ants. The ants fight off enemies.

In Australia, the ant-house plant provides a "house" for ants in its large stem. The ants' waste products provide the plant with food!

▲ Some ants live in the acacia tree's hollow thorns. The adult ants eat the plant's nectar and their young feed on the tips of the leaves. In return, the ants attack plant-eating insects.

OTHER Ant Partners

Some ants and aphids live together in harmony. The aphids provide the ants with honeydew, a sweet liquid they produce. In return, the ants guard the aphids' young and even carry them to new plants.

In the rain forest, fig wasps and fig trees have an amazing partnership. The fig wasps make sure that the fruit of the fig tree ripens. The wasps enter the small opening in the fig and **pollinate** the flowers that are hidden inside the unripe figs.

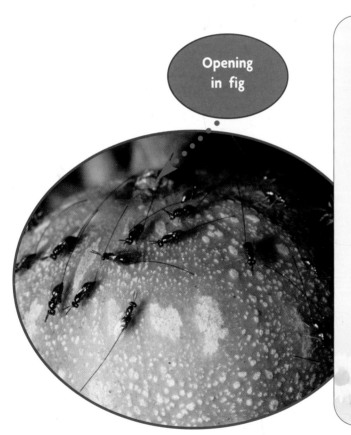

Opening in fig

OTHER Wasp Partners

Sometimes, wasp partnerships are one-sided. A certain kind of wasp lays its eggs in the body of another animal, such as a caterpillar. When the eggs hatch, the larvae feed on the caterpillar's body from the inside. Eventually, the caterpillar dies.

▲ This drawing shows the leaves and seeds of a fig tree.

HOW Do Plants and Mammals Help Each Other?

Oak trees help squirrels by providing them with acorns to eat. And although the squirrel doesn't know it, it helps the oak trees by "planting" new trees.

▼ This squirrel is eating an acorn.

▲ This squirrel is burying an acorn.

In the late summer and fall, squirrels store acorns for winter. Sometimes, they forget where they have buried them, and the acorns begin to grow. In time, a **seedling** pops out of the ground. Over the years, the seedling grows into a tall, leafy oak tree.

Many mammals, such as zebras and antelope, live on the grasslands of Africa. Both these animals are partners with the grass plants they eat. In a surprising way, they actually help the grass grow!

▼ The grasslands of Africa are home to zebras and antelopes. The animals' partnership with the grass plants they eat helps the plants grow.

When the animals eat grass, they bite off the top part of the grass plant. They leave the bottom part of the plant in the ground. The bottom part is where the plant's **shoots**, or new leaves and roots, grow from. When the tops of the grass plants are bitten off, the shoots get more sunlight and grow better.

OTHER Zebra Partners

Zebras also partner with other animals. In Africa, a bird called the oxpecker feeds on the ticks that live on the zebra's skin. The zebra benefits from a tick-free skin, and the oxpecker uses some of the zebra's hair to line its nest.

◀ grass plant and its shoots

How Do Plants and Sea Animals Help Each Other?

Tiny sea animals called coral polyps build coral reefs. They are partners with tiny plants that live inside their bodies. Without each other, both organisms would die.

▲ A coral polyp has a soft body with a hard skeleton around it. These coral polyps are called Cup Coral polyps.

Each polyp forms a hard skeleton around its soft, jellylike body. Over many years, the skeletons of millions of polyps form the coral reef.

This is a Cup Coral reef. ▼

The tiny plants that live in the jellylike bodies of the coral polyps produce wastes and gases that the coral polyps use for food and breathing. At the same time, the coral polyps help the plants survive by providing a place to live.

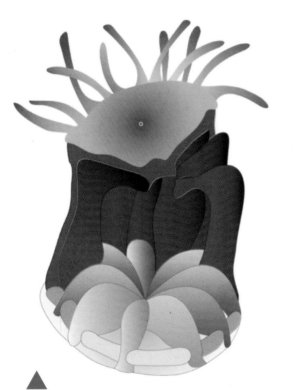

OTHER Sea Animal Partners

Fish, crabs, and other sea creatures make their homes among the coral reefs. Some form partnerships with other animals. As the name suggests, cleaner fish clean bigger fish. They get a meal, and the other fish are kept clean.

▲ Coral polyps and their plant partners can only survive in shallow waters. This is because the plants need sunlight to make food. The plants that live inside the body of a coral polyp give the animal its color.

connect these animals to their plant partners?

squirrel

fig tree

parrot

flower

ant

fruit plant

bee

oak tree

fig wasp

grass

zebra

sea plant

coral polyp

acacia tree

Glossary

algae (AL-jee): plantlike organisms that use sunlight to make food

coral polyp (KOHR-uhl PAH-lihp): a small sea animal that has a jellylike body and a hard skeleton

food chain (FOOD CHAYNE): the food and energy links between the different plants and animals living in the same place

nectar (NEHK-ter): the sweet liquid inside many flowers

pollen (PAH-lihn): the yellow, dusty powder that a plant needs to make seeds

pollinate (PAH-lih-nayt): to spread pollen from flower to flower

seedling (SEED-lihng): a young plant

shoot (SHOOT): a new leaf and root of a plant

Index